S0-BAT-728

LIVING IN THE WILD: PRIMATES

ORANGUTANS

Buffy Silverman

Heinemann
LIBRARY

Chicago, Illinois

www.capstonepub.com
Visit our website to find out more information about Heinemann-Raintree books.

To order:

☎ Phone 888-454-2279

💻 Visit www.capstonepub.com to browse our catalog and order online.

© 2012 Heinemann Library
an imprint of Capstone Global Library, LLC
Chicago, Illinois

All rights reserved. No part of this publication may be reproduced or transmitted in any form or by any means, electronic or mechanical, including photocopying, recording, taping, or any information storage and retrieval system, without permission in writing from the publisher.

Edited by Abby Colich, Jilly Hunt, and Vaarunika Dharmapala
Designed by Victoria Allen
Picture research by Tracy Cummins
Original illustrations © Capstone Global Library Ltd 2012
Illustrations by Oxford Designers & Illustrators and HL Studios

Originated by Capstone Global Library Ltd
Printed and bound in China by CTPS

15 14 13 12 11
10 9 8 7 6 5 4 3 2 1

Library of Congress Cataloging-in-Publication Data
Silverman, Buffy.
  Orangutans / Buffy Silverman.—1st ed.
    p. cm.—(Living in the wild. Primates)
  Includes bibliographical references and index.
  ISBN 978-1-4329-5866-4 (hb)—ISBN 978-1-4329-5873-2 (pb) 1. Orangutan—Juvenile literature. I. Title.
  QL737.P96S55 2012
  599.88'3—dc22   2011012899

Acknowledgments
We would like to thank the following for permission to reproduce photographs: AP Photo p. 5 (Binsar Bakkara); Corbis pp. 13 (© Wayne Lawler/Ecoscene), 36 (© Stringer/Indonesia/Reuters), 37 (© Chaiwat Subprasom/Reuters); Fame Pictures p. 31 (Barcroft); FLPA pp. 21 (Suzi Eszterhas/Minden Pictures), 22 (Cyril Ruoso/Minden Pictures), 23 (Gerry Ellis/Minden Pictures), 29 (Thomas Marent/Minden Pictures), 44 (Frans Lanting); Getty Images p. 33 (Suzanne Plunkett); istockphoto pp. 19 (© Jeryl Tan), 39 (© Anthony Brown); National Geographic Stock pp. 18 (Ch'ien Lee/Minden Pictures), 43 (S. Janssen/Foto Natura/Minden); Photolibrary pp. 16 (Arouse Arouse), 27 (Avisage Avisage); Photoshot p. 15 (NPHA), 30 (NPHA); Rex USA p. 41; Shutterstock pp. 6 (© Michael Lynch), 7 (© iPics), 8 (© javarman), 11 (© Stéphane Bidouze), 14 (© Uryadnikov Sergey), 20 (© Uryadnikov Sergey), 25 (© Ronald van der Beek), 26 (© Uryadnikov Sergey), 34 (© A.S. Zain), 35 (© think4photop).

Cover photograph of a baby orangutan at Tanjung Puting National Park, Borneo, reproduced with permission of Photolibrary (Theo Allofs).

Every effort has been made to contact copyright holders of any material reproduced in this book. Any omissions will be rectified in subsequent printings if notice is given to the publisher.

Disclaimer
All the Internet addresses (URLs) given in this book were valid at the time of going to press. However, due to the dynamic nature of the Internet, some addresses may have changed, or sites may have changed or ceased to exist since publication. While the author and publisher regret any inconvenience this may cause readers, no responsibility for any such changes can be accepted by either the author or the publisher.

Contents

Some words are shown in bold, **like this**. You can find out what they mean by looking in the glossary.

What Are Primates?

An orangutan sits high up in a tree. She spies fruit hanging nearby and grabs a branch. She swings toward the fruit. Her long arms span the gaps between the branches. She reaches her goal and eats.

Primates are a group of **mammals** that includes orangutans, monkeys, apes, and people. Lemurs, lorises, bush babies, and tarsiers are primates, too. There are more than 350 different kinds of primates.

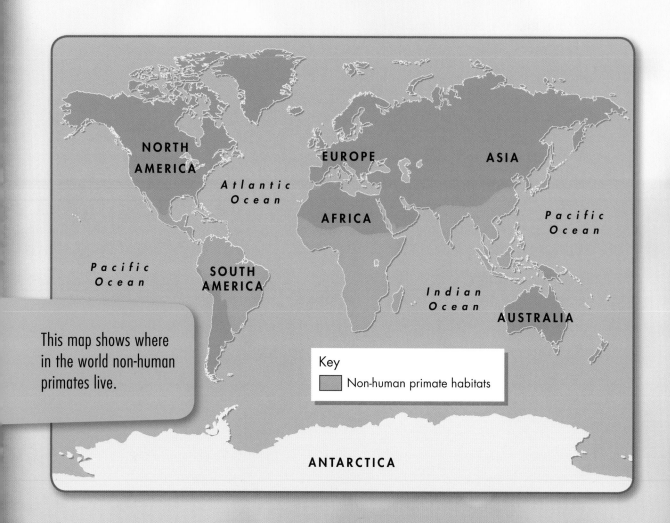

This map shows where in the world non-human primates live.

NORTH AMERICA

Atlantic Ocean

EUROPE

ASIA

AFRICA

Pacific Ocean

Pacific Ocean

SOUTH AMERICA

Indian Ocean

AUSTRALIA

Key
Non-human primate habitats

ANTARCTICA

Like all mammals, primates have fur and feed their babies milk. They breathe air and keep a constantly warm body temperature. Primates give birth to live babies and care for their young.

Living in trees

Many primates live in trees. Instead of paws, primates have hands and feet. Their five-fingered hands are useful for gripping tree branches. Touch the thumb of your right hand to the fingers of your right hand. You can do this because, like most primates, you have **opposable thumbs**. That means the thumbs can be placed opposite the fingers on the same hand.

Opposable thumbs allow primates to pick up tiny objects. When a primate sits, its hands are free. Primates grab food with their hands and put it in their mouths. The sensitive tips of their fingers can feel different objects. Most primates grip with their feet, too. Their big toes are like thumbs that help them climb and grasp.

This baby orangutan is playing with her keeper at a rescue center in Indonesia.

Hands and feet

Primates have other **adaptations** that help them make good use of their hands and feet. Instead of claws, primates have flat nails on their thumbs. Some have nails on all their fingers and toes. Their nails allow them to pick up objects more easily than they could with claws.

Primates can twist their hands and feet in many directions. Two bones in their lower arms and legs allow them to do this. Many animals, such as dogs and cats, walk on their toes. Primates walk on flat feet and can stand or walk upright.

The pygmy marmoset is one of the smallest primates in the world. It weighs about as much as a large candy bar!

Seeing the world

Primates have forward-facing eyes and excellent depth perception. This means that they can see three-dimensional (3–D) shapes and can judge distances. Primates know how far to reach for the next branch because of their depth perception. They depend more on their sense of sight than on their sense of smell. Because most primates rely less on their sense of smell than other mammals, they have smaller, flattened noses.

Gorillas are the largest primates in the world. An adult male gorilla can weigh more than twice as much as a human man.

Primates are intelligent, large-brained animals. They often live together in groups. They protect their young and teach them the skills they will need as adults. Young primates take a long time to grow up. While they are growing, they depend on their mothers for food and protection. Primates grow up slowly, but they live for a long time.

What Are Orangutans?

Orangutans swing from branch to branch, high up in the trees. They scramble up and down tree trunks, and they reach from one tree to the next. They are as acrobatic as circus performers! Grabbing onto vines and branches, they travel across the forest.

Orangutans' arms stretch out longer than the length of their bodies. A male orangutan's reach can span almost 8 feet (2.5 meters). Orangutans can grasp branches with their hands and feet and can hang upside-down while snacking on fruit. With their long arms and short legs, they move slowly and awkwardly on the ground. Up in the trees, they can move gracefully.

Orangutans can reach easily from branch to branch.

Person of the forest

Orangutan means "person of the forest" in Malay. Malay is one of the languages spoken in Borneo and Sumatra (see map below). Orangutans live in the **tropical** forests on these islands.

Orangutans are the largest tree-living animals. Males weigh up to 300 pounds (136 kilograms). Adult males live alone. They make loud calls that tell other males to stay away. They also grow big cheek pads called flanges. These cheek pads show that they are fully grown and ready to fight other males that come too close. Female orangutans are much smaller and weigh less than half a male's weight. They live with their young.

Orangutans spend most of their day eating and resting in trees. Every night, they weave nests of leaves and branches to sleep in. Their red fur is easy to spot in the open. In the shadows of the forest, they stay hidden.

Orangutans live on the islands of Borneo and Sumatra in Southeast Asia.

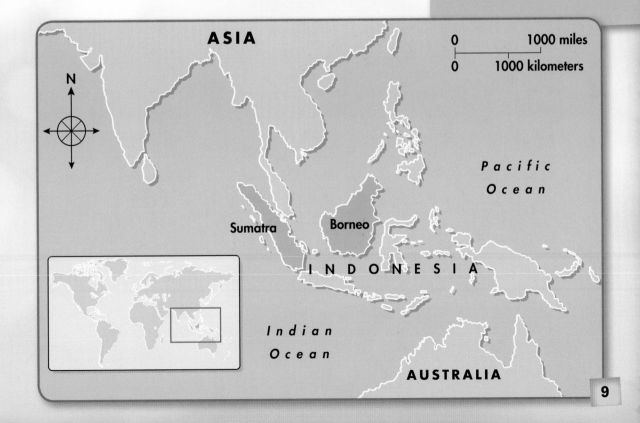

9

How Are Orangutans Classified?

When scientists **classify** living things, they place them in groups. **Mammals** are divided into many smaller groups. One of these is primates. Primates are further divided into six groups: lemurs; lorises, pottos, and bush babies; tarsiers, New World monkeys; Old World monkeys; and apes. Orangutans are a kind of ape.

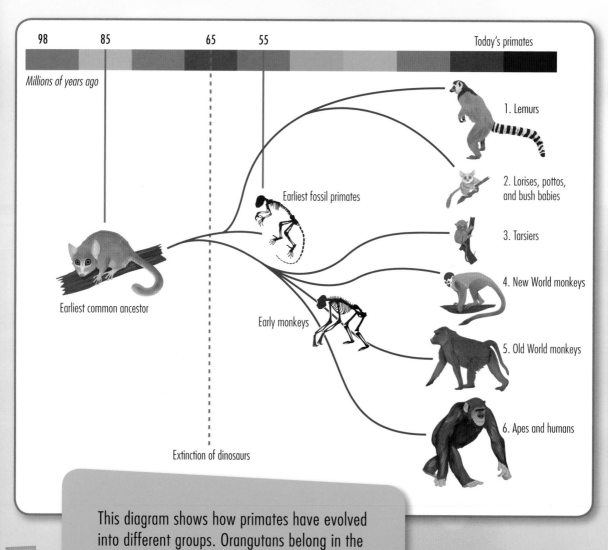

98   85   65   55   Today's primates

Millions of years ago

Earliest fossil primates

1. Lemurs

2. Lorises, pottos, and bush babies

3. Tarsiers

4. New World monkeys

5. Old World monkeys

6. Apes and humans

Earliest common ancestor

Early monkeys

Extinction of dinosaurs

This diagram shows how primates have evolved into different groups. Orangutans belong in the same group as apes and humans.

Meet the apes

Orangutans, gorillas, chimpanzees, bonobos, and humans belong to a group within the apes called the great apes. Orangutans split off from other great apes about 12 to 15 million years ago. They are the only great apes in Asia. The other great apes are found in Africa and are more closely related to each other than they are to orangutans.

There are two different **species** of orangutan. They **evolved** into separate species 500,000 to 2.3 million years ago. The two species live on different islands. Bornean orangutans live only on the island of Borneo. Sumatran orangutans live only on the neighboring island of Sumatra.

TWO SPECIES

Sumatran orangutans are thinner and have longer fur than their Bornean relatives. The males' cheek pads are also narrower than Bornean males' cheek pads.

Sumatran orangutans have long beards and long faces.

Where Do Orangutans Live?

The place where a living thing makes its home is called its **habitat**. Thousands of years ago, orangutan habitats spread across southern China and Southeast Asia. Hundreds of thousands of orangutans lived in these forests. Their **fossils** have been found in Java, Thailand, Malaysia, Vietnam, and China (see map below).

Today, orangutans are **extinct** in all these places. There are now fewer than 60,000 orangutans alive.

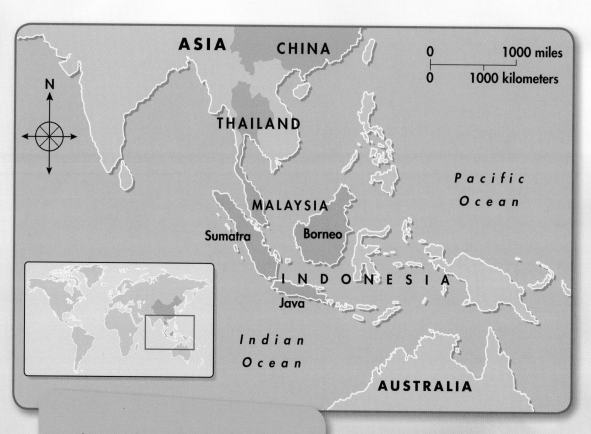

This map shows where orangutan fossils have been found. Compare it to the map on page 9. You can see how orangutan habitats have shrunk.

Island homes

In the past, **tropical rain forests** covered most of Sumatra. Orangutans lived across the island until humans cleared much of the forest. Today, Sumatran orangutans are found only on the northern tip of the island. They live in swampy low forests and in mountainous tropical forests. Rain falls in Sumatra for nine months of the year. It is warm and humid all year long. A large variety of trees and other plants grow in the forests.

Bornean orangutans live on the island of Borneo. Borneo is the third-largest island in the world. Its forests are also warm and humid. Orangutans live in eight different regions across Borneo in hilly tropical forests and swampy low forests. A thick soil called peat covers the moist ground. Dark, slow-moving rivers run through the forests.

Orangutans depend on fruit that grows in forests. They travel from tree to tree, searching for fruit. Occasionally they wander into grasslands, fields, gardens, and lakes.

Many orangutans live in tropical forests like this one.

What Adaptations Help Orangutans Survive?

Imagine trying to swing from one forest tree to another, without climbing down to the ground. You would need balance and strength to hold onto the branches. Excellent vision would help you judge the distances between branches. You would need to decide the best path across long distances. You would rely on your intelligence to plan your route.

An **adaptation** is a characteristic that helps a living thing survive in its **habitat**. Living things **evolve** adaptations over many generations. Adaptations can help animals find food, find a mate, or swing in the treetops. An adaptation can also help them escape predators (animals that hunt other animals). Orangutans have many adaptations that allow them to live in their forest homes.

Strong arms allow orangutans to swing from branches and climb up trees.

Holding on

Long arms, short legs, and grasping feet make an orangutan awkward on the ground. However, in the safety of the trees, these characteristics are an advantage. An orangutan's long arms allow it to move hand over hand, reaching and grabbing for the next branch.

An orangutan uses its feet like an extra pair of hands as it climbs up and down tree trunks. Curved fingers and toes act like hooks for hanging from branches. Short, **opposable thumbs** and big toes let the animal grasp tightly and stay put. A young orangutan uses its strong grasp to cling to its mother's fur while she climbs in the trees.

An orangutan can rotate and move its shoulder and hip joints more than a person can. This gives an orangutan the flexibility to move easily from branch to branch. An orangutan is so flexible that it can rest with a leg behind its head!

Orangutans can grasp with their feet as well as their hands.

Staying safe

An orangutan's ability to move through trees helps it to avoid many predators. Its red coat blends in with the shady forest, keeping it hidden. By living alone or in small groups, orangutans are less likely to be spotted.

Find out what this orangutan is up to by reading the next page.

TIGERS!

In Sumatra, where tigers hunt on the ground, orangutans rarely climb out of trees. In Borneo, there are no tigers. Bornean orangutans climb down to the ground more often.

Finding and eating food

Orangutans' complex brains make them highly intelligent and well adapted to their forest homes. They learn and remember where their favorite trees are and they know when different fruits ripen. Orangutans also know how tools can help them get food. They stick branches into bees' nests and pull out honey or dig for termites in the ground (see the photograph on page 16). When fruit is too far away to grab, orangutans use sticks to pull it toward them. Orangutans also have adaptations that help them eat the food they find. Their strong teeth and jaws help them to crush nuts and chew thick leaves.

Good eyesight also helps orangutans to find food in shady forests. Color vision helps them recognize ripe fruit. Because orangutans have eyes that face forward, the view from one eye overlaps with the view from the other eye. This is called binocular vision. It allows orangutans to see a three-dimensional (3-D) image, so they can judge the distance from one branch to another. They know exactly when to grasp and when to let go.

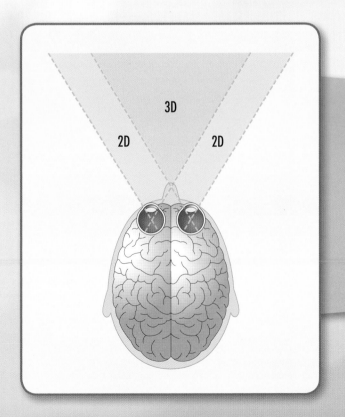

In binocular vision, both eyes have an overlapped view of an object. This three-dimensional view is important for judging depth.

What Do Orangutans Eat?

A cricket chews leaves in a **rain forest**. A young orangutan grabs the cricket and swallows. As night falls, a leopard watches the orangutan. It pounces from a tree branch, killing the young orangutan.

The tree, cricket, orangutan, and leopard are all part of a rain forest food chain. A food chain is made up of a series of living things that are each dependent on the next as a source of food.

Pythons prey on young orangutans.

Many food chains

Orangutans eat many different foods, so they are part of many food chains. They eat over 400 different kinds of plants. Their diet consists mainly of fruit. Sumatran orangutans especially enjoy figs. They move from place to place as different fruits ripen. When there is not enough ripe fruit and nuts, orangutans also eat buds, flowers, leaves, bark, sap, and plant roots. They snack on insects, including termites, ants, and crickets. They eat bird eggs, mushrooms, and honey. Occasionally orangutans hunt small **mammals**. They reach into tree holes to find lorises that sleep during the day.

Orangutans spit out fruit seeds. Seeds also go through their digestive system and come out as waste. In this way, orangutans spread seeds throughout the rain forest, and soon new seedlings grow.

An orangutan pries open the tough outside of a durian fruit.

What Is an Orangutan's Life Cycle?

A baby orangutan holds onto its mother's belly. With its fingers and toes, it clings to the mother's fur. Like all **mammals**, an orangutan depends on its mother when it is young. It becomes more independent as it grows and matures.

An animal's life cycle is the series of stages that it passes through as it grows and develops from a single cell into an adult. Orangutans have one of the slowest life cycles of any mammal. The life cycle begins with mating. A male's sperm joins with a female's egg and fertilizes it. This means that the egg is now ready to grow. The fertilized egg divides and grows inside the mother. A mother orangutan is pregnant for eight and a half months before giving birth. Usually a mother orangutan gives birth to only one baby. Twins occur rarely.

A young orangutan learns about the world while clinging to its mother.

Baby orangutans

A newborn orangutan is tiny and helpless. It weighs 3 to 4½ pounds (1½ to 2 kilograms). Mother orangutans take good care of their babies. The father has no part in the care. The mother carries her baby through the treetops and feeds it milk. The baby sleeps in the mother's nest. For the first four months of its life, the baby clings to its mother's belly. Gradually, it learns to climb up and ride on its mother's back.

A young orangutan tastes soft food from its mother's lips at about four months old. It begins to eat many new foods. When a young orangutan is about four, its mother stops feeding it with her milk.

This baby orangutan is playing near its mother's nest.

Growing up

From the age of two, young orangutans climb through the trees, holding hands with other orangutans. From ages two to five, they take short trips away from their mothers while staying in sight. They follow their mothers as they move through the trees. If a gap between branches is too wide, the mothers make bridges with their bodies. Then the young orangutans can scramble across.

As they grow, orangutans spend more time away from their mothers. They travel and play with each other, but they still have contact with their mothers. Around the age of eight, orangutans leave their mothers. They then often travel around with other young orangutans.

This mother orangutan is making a bridge for her baby with her body.

Becoming an adult

Young female orangutans live near their mothers. They mate with whichever male defends the area where they feed. Females give birth for the first time between the ages of 14 and 15. A mother orangutan gives birth once every eight years. This is the longest time between births of any mammal. During her lifetime, a female orangutan has four or five babies.

Young male orangutans wander from place to place when they are 8 to 15 years old. They are able to mate, but females are unlikely to choose them. Females look for adult males that have cheek pads. Males try to mate with any females in their home range.

Orangutans live for about 35 to 40 years in the wild. In captivity, some live to be 50 years old or more.

Orangutans learn by playing with each other.

How Do Orangutans Behave?

Most great apes live in groups, but orangutans do not. Adult males live alone, while female orangutans stay with their young. Young males and females that have left their mothers sometimes form small groups. These groups break apart by the time the members become adults.

An adult male has a large home range. The male travels around this area, moving to where fruit is ripe. Heavy males do not swing easily on tree branches. They sometimes climb to the ground.

Fight or flight?

Males make a rumbling, howling call. Even in dense **rain forests**, the loud call carries for almost a mile (over a kilometer). The call lasts for one to two minutes. When younger males hear it, they run away. If two males meet each other, a fight may occur, especially if a female is nearby. The larger male grabs and bites the other's cheek pads. Many adult males have scars or are missing fingers from these battles.

Females find mates by listening to long calls. After mating, the male and female may travel together for a few days or weeks. If a female has a baby, it travels along with the pair.

LOW ENERGY

A study has found that orangutans need less food, weight for weight, than humans and most other **mammals**. Because of their low energy needs, they can survive when food is scarce. They also grow and reproduce slowly.

A male's cheek pads show that he is an adult.

Several females usually live in the same area as a male. Females meet each other while looking for food. They may ignore each other or be friendly. Where fruit is plentiful, groups of orangutans feed near each other and travel together.

Daily life

Orangutans spend most of their days feeding, resting, and moving between their feeding and resting spots. Early in the morning, an orangutan spends two or three hours feeding. In the middle of the day, the orangutan rests. Then it feeds again in the afternoon. In the evening, it travels to a tree, where it will sleep for the night.

An orangutan seems to think and observe before it acts. It will stare at fruit before climbing over to pick it. Unlike other primates, orangutans do not spend all of their time looking for food. They often stay in one place for a long time. Sometimes orangutans study others and then try to copy them. Orangutans that have watched people in a boat may get on board when the boat is empty. They paddle it with their hands!

This orangutan is paddling across a river!

Nest building

Every night, an orangutan builds a new nest in a tree. It stacks branches with leaves in a pile. In a few minutes, the nest is finished. Sometimes an orangutan will use an old nest. If it is raining, it will add a cover of large leaves to help it stay dry. Orangutans also make day nests for their naps, but these are less sturdy.

A baby orangutan sleeps in its mother's nest. The baby watches when its mother builds a nest. By the age of two, the young orangutan begins to make practice nests during playtime. At the age of five, it builds its own nest and sleeps alone.

Would *you* like to sleep in a nest high above the ground?

A DAY IN THE LIFE OF AN ORANGUTAN

Young orangutans learn and practice new skills as they follow their mothers. They learn where to find food, what to eat, how to use tools, and how to build nests. The story that follows depicts a typical day, from sunrise to sunset.

High in the canopy of a Bornean rain forest, a young orangutan sleeps. She lies safely in the nest she shares with her mother. As the sun rises, she wakes. She drinks her mother's milk then climbs out of the nest, ready to start her day. She follows her mother, swinging hand-over-hand, crossing to a tree that is heavy with fruit. They start to eat.

Two other young orangutans and their mother come to eat fruit. One is a tiny baby, clinging to the fur on her mother's belly. The other is almost fully grown. The youngsters chase each other through the branches.

Suddenly, our young orangutan hears her mother making kissing sounds. She shakes a tree branch and throws twigs. The young orangutan scrambles over and clutches her mother's fur. A python slithers on a branch below. Both mothers lead their young away.

Rain begins to fall. The orangutans pick leafy branches and cover their heads. Our youngster clings to her mother, staying dry during the downpour.

After an afternoon nap, the young orangutan and her mother set off again. Her mother breaks off a dead tree limb and hands her a piece of damp wood. She pries it open and finds termites to eat.

Soon it is time to build a nest for the night. The young orangutan watches her mother stacking branches. She also adds branches and piles on leaves. She has been practicing nest building since she was little, and she knows how to make her own nest. But for now she sleeps with her mother. She yawns. After a long day of swinging and eating, she is ready to sleep.

A baby orangutan stays close to her mother.
A young female orangutan has joined them.

How Intelligent Are Orangutans?

You would not want to hold a spiky durian fruit in your bare hands. Some orangutans have found a way to open the prickly fruit without harming themselves. They stack a pile of leaves and use them like gloves. This keeps their hands safe.

Like other great apes, orangutans are very intelligent. They make and use tools to get food and water. They pry open fruits and seed pods with sticks. They poke sticks into tree holes and pull out insects or honey. They scoop water out of tree holes with leafy branches. They chew leaves to make a sponge that soaks up water from tree holes.

This orangutan is trying to stay dry under an umbrella of leaves.

Tool use

Just like humans, orangutans use tools to make themselves comfortable—and for fun. When bees or wasps fly around, orangutans swat them away with leafy branches. During a rainstorm, orangutans hold up large leaves and use them like an umbrella. They also drape leafy branches over themselves and wear them like ponchos. When the sun is bright, they shade themselves with leaves. An orangutan with an itch will use a branch to scratch itself.

How do orangutans know how to make and use tools? They watch and learn from other orangutans. Different groups of orangutans use tools in different ways. For example, orangutans in one group use leaves as napkins to wipe off sticky substances from their faces. Those in another group hold leaves up to their mouths to make loud sounds before they settle into their nests.

This orangutan is using a stick to spear a fish.

Teaching and learning

Humans spend many years going to school, learning different skills. Orangutans need to learn many skills, too. Mothers teach their young where to find food and how to eat it. Orangutans learn to recognize hundreds of different foods. They have a mental map of where trees with certain fruits grow. They know which fruits ripen during different seasons. Young orangutans learn how to make tools that help them to get food. They learn how to make nests and how to stay safe.

People have taught orangutans in captivity many things. Orangutans can learn human sign language. They know how to play computer games with touch screens. They stack boxes to make ladders and connect sticks together for extending their reach. They make swings from ropes and use sticks to dig holes.

BIRUTÉ MARY GALDIKAS

For the past 40 years, Biruté Mary Galdikas has observed orangutans in Borneo. She was the first researcher to realize how long a period of time passed between orangutan births. She observed orangutans eating over 400 different foods, and she has learned about orangutan social and mating systems. In addition to teaching people about orangutans, Galdikas has worked hard to protect orangutan **habitats**.

Biruté Mary Galdikas sits with an orangutan at a research center in Indonesia.

What Threats Do Orangutans Face?

Orangutans are in trouble. Bornean orangutans are **endangered**. Scientists believe there is a high risk that the orangutans will become **extinct** in the wild. In 2004, scientists estimated that there were between 45,000 and 69,000 orangutans in Borneo. Fifty years earlier, there were more than twice that many.

The future is even more uncertain for Sumatran orangutans. They are considered critically endangered. "Critically endangered" means they face a very high risk of becoming extinct in the near future. The Sumatran orangutan could be the first great ape to become extinct in recorded history. As of 2004, there were only 7,300 orangutans in Sumatra. Seventy-five years earlier, there were about five times as many. The orangutan populations in Borneo and Sumatra are almost certainly smaller today than they were in 2004.

Logging in rain forests destroys orangutan **habitats**.

Disappearing forests

Why is the number of orangutans falling? The **tropical rain forests** where they live are being destroyed. Orangutans are born, grow up, find food, sleep, and mate in trees. They cannot survive without forests. Sumatran orangutans rarely leave the treetops. Bornean orangutans spend most of their time in trees. Without large areas of forests, both groups of orangutans will suffer.

Oil palm trees

People are responsible for the destruction of the Sumatran and Bornean rain forests. Huge areas of forests have been cleared and planted with oil palm trees. People use palm oil in many foods, in soaps, and in detergents. Many countries also want to use palm oil as a biofuel. Biofuels are fuels made from plants and animal waste.

These are the seeds of oil palm trees.

Other land uses

The demand for palm oil around the world is growing. More than 500,000 square miles (129,000 square kilometers) of the world's rain forests have been turned into oil palm plantations.

Crops such as rice and cocoa are planted on land that was once forest. Forests have also been cleared to build roads and cities and to mine gold.

The moisture in the soil once controlled forest fires in Borneo and Sumatra. When forests are logged, the soil becomes drier. Branches and leaves that are left behind after logging can catch fire. People also set fires to clear land for oil palm trees. Huge forest fires kill orangutans and destroy their habitat.

Fire can destroy large areas of rain forest.

Poaching

Illegal hunting, called poaching, also threatens orangutans. Orangutans move slowly, making them an easy target. Hunters kill adult female orangutans and capture their young. They sell baby orangutans as pets. In the past, hunting has led to whole groups of orangutans becoming extinct.

Until recently, people had little impact on the rain forests of Borneo and Sumatra. They did not compete with orangutans for their forest homes. Now that situation has changed. People use more and more materials from rain forests. As a result, orangutan habitats have declined by 80 percent in the last 20 years. Less than 2 percent of the rain forest is protected. For orangutans to survive, they need large reserves and wildlife protection laws. Most of all, people need ways of making a living that do not harm rain forests.

It is hard for young orangutans to survive without their mothers.

How Can People Help Orangutans?

There are many reasons to care about orangutans and their forest homes. They are the only great apes left in Asia. The ways in which they eat, sleep, and travel among the treetops set them apart from other great apes, too.

Watch an orangutan making tools or building a nest and you might be reminded of human behavior. Orangutans are closely related to us. They share about 97 percent of their **genes** with humans.

Protecting orangutans and rain forests

Orangutans play an important role in keeping **rain forests** healthy. By eating fruits, they spread seeds, so new plants can grow. Other animals need these plants in order to survive.

When people protect the forests that orangutans depend on, they protect thousands of other **species**, too. Many of these plants and animals are found nowhere else on Earth. Proboscis monkeys, hornbills, gibbons, Sumatran tigers, and cloud leopards are just a few of them.

People also benefit from rain forests. Many medicines are made from rain forest plants. These plants may hold new cures for diseases. They will not be found if forests are burned or chopped down. Rain forests soak up rain, so the land does not flood. Clean water flows through them, and forest plants clean the air. Some kinds of fish that people eat breed in forest wetlands.

IAN SINGLETON

Ian Singleton spent more than two years living in the swamps of Sumatra, studying orangutans. He is now the scientific director for the Sumatran Orangutan Conservation Program. This program **reintroduces** Sumatran orangutans to protected forests in the southern part of the island. If these orangutans survive and have babies, it will help maintain their numbers in the wild.

These orangutans are being fed by their keepers at a sanctuary in Borneo.

Conservation

Without human help, orangutan numbers will continue to decline as their forest homes disappear. **Conserving** the rain forest is a huge challenge, but many people are trying to meet it. Local governments in Indonesia are working to save forests. They try to teach people how rain forests help them, so that local people will want to save the forests. They try to stop illegal logging and building in forests.

People are also trying to find different ways to grow oil palm trees. Instead of clearing more rain forest land, trees can be planted on land that is no longer being used for crops. By finding better ways to grow oil palm trees, forests can be conserved. Groups are encouraging palm oil companies to save wildlife near their plantations. Others are asking their governments to decrease the amount of biofuels they plan to use, until trees can be grown in a way that does not harm more rain forests.

PALM OIL PRESSURE

Golden Agri-Resources is the world's second-biggest palm oil company. In 2011 it announced plans to stop cutting down certain rain forests. It promised to protect lands that are important to orangutans and other animals. Many conservation groups pressured Golden Agri-Resources to make this promise. Some food companies even said they would not buy palm oil from companies that destroyed the rain forest.

You can help orangutans!

How can you help orangutans? Teach others about orangutans and the dangers they face. Many organizations work to help orangutans and save their homes. Raise money and donate it to one of these groups, such as the World Wildlife Fund or the Orangutan Conservancy. Perhaps you could "adopt" an orangutan through the Orangutan Foundation International.

A young orangutan plays with a ranger at a Bornean nature reserve.

What Does the Future Hold for Orangutans?

Without **rain forests** in Borneo and Sumatra, orangutans cannot survive. As more and more **tropical** rain forests are cleared for other uses, orangutans have become rare. Unless people take action to save their **habitats**, orangutans may soon become **extinct**.

Many groups work to protect orangutans. They fight to protect the remaining rain forests. They replant forests that have been logged. They try to protect orangutans from being hunted.

Many people who hunt and trade orangutans have no other source of income. By helping them find another way to earn a living, orangutans can be saved. One way people who live near orangutans can make a living is through **eco-tourism**. Travelers from around the world visit Borneo and Sumatra to see orangutans. As more and more people become aware of the orangutans' plight, they will join the fight to save their habitat.

No one knows what the future holds for orangutans. But many people are working to make sure that orangutans and their rain forest homes will survive.

TANJUNG PUTING NATIONAL PARK

Tanjung Puting National Park in Borneo is home to the largest remaining group of wild orangutans. However, 12 million acres (50,000 square kilometers) of oil palm plantations are planned for areas near the park. Because of this, many people are concerned about the future of this important orangutan habitat.

It is important that we do not allow orangutans to die out. We can protect these amazing primates and their habitats.

Orangutan Profile

long arms

forward-facing eyes

grasping feet

opposable thumb

Species: *Pongo abelii* (Sumatran orangutan) and *Pongo pygmaeus* (Bornean orangutan)

Weight: Adult males, 110 to 300 pounds (50 to 136 kilograms); adult females, 30 to 50 kilograms (66 to 110 pounds)

Height [from head to rump]: Adult males, 40 inches (102 centimeters); adult females, 30 inches (76 centimeters)

Habitat: Rain forests

Diet: Fruits, leaves, shoots, flowers, bark, ants, termites, bird eggs, and small **mammals**

Number of young: 4 to 5 infants after 8½ months of pregnancy. Females will give birth about every 8 years, after they have reached maturity at 14 to 15 years old.

Birth weight: 3.3 to 4.5 pounds (1.5 to 2 kilograms)

Life expectancy: 30 to 40 years in the wild, and 50 years or longer in captivity

Glossary

adaptation body part or behavior of a living thing that helps it survive in a particular habitat

classify group living things together by their similarities and differences

conserve protect from harm or destruction

eco-tourism form of tourism to observe wildlife and help protect nature

endangered living thing that is at risk of dying out

evolve change gradually over time

extinct living thing that has died out

fossil remains of living things preserved in rock and other materials

gene information that is passed from parent to young that determines species, as well as other characteristics

habitat natural environment of a living thing

mammal animal that has fur or hair, gives birth to live young, and feeds its young on milk from the mother

opposable thumb thumb that can face and touch the fingers on the same hand

rain forest forest with tall, thickly growing trees in an area with high rainfall

reintroduce put a living thing back into its natural environment

species group of similar living things that can mate with each other

tropical regions of Earth around the equator

Find Out More

Books

de la Bedoyere, Camilla. *100 Things You Should Know About Monkeys and Apes*. New York: Barnes and Noble, 2008.

Moore, Heidi. *Protecting Food Chains: Rain Forest Food Chains*. Chicago: Heinemann Library, 2011.

Solway, Andrew. *Classifying Living Things: Classifying Mammals*. Chicago: Heinemann Library, 2009.

Websites

www.orangutan.org
Find out more about orangutans and how people can help protect them at this website.

http://kids.nationalgeographic.com/kids/animals/creaturefeature/ orangutan/
Learn about orangutans at this website, which includes videos.

Organizations to contact

Orangutan Conservancy
www.orangutan.com
This organization aims to help save orangutans from extinction.

World Wildlife Fund
www.wwf.org
WWF works to protect animals and nature.

Endangered Species International
www.endangeredspeciesinternational.org/index.php
This organization focuses on saving endangered animals around the world.

Index